HELLISH WORLD

POEMS AND QUOTES

SHREERAJ MENON

Contents

Contents

Contents

Contents

Contents

Preface

This book consists of some of the poems and Quotes written by the author on the theme of Love, Nature and general day to day aspects of life. There are some inspirational quotes too. Love includes Love found, Love lost and love re-awakened. Similarly, Nature consists of the importance of nature and how people mis-utilize the nature to their own advantages without going for the aftereffects. General consists of the general aspects of life which goes on with people and the surroundings.

Acknowledgements

I would like to thank my friends who inspired me in writing the Poems and Quotes which I used to say out and forget it. I would also like to thank Your Quote platforms and all its members and groups for allowing me and inspiring me to write my contents on its platform. I would also like to thank Notion Press and all its members who allowed me to publish my contents through their platform and the time-to-time guidance which they gave me to correct my errors.

1. Gratitude

Gratitude

The blessings of the universe which I have
Making my day as bright and thrive

Feeling of being myself with the nature
Nurtures my life beautiful and more azure

The love which you gave me all the while
I thank you my universe with a smile

Letting go off the past which is not needed
Moving with positivity and good things ahead

My guardian angels and archangels helps me
From the hurdles by a shield protecting me

I thank you very much for being with me from the start
Giving my gratitude from the bottom of my heart
---Shreeraj Menon

— Raj

2. A beautiful lesson from life

YourQuote.in
A beautiful lesson from life is

A beautiful lesson from life is
Never to trust your shadows
There are people that breaks
Your heart and leave in sorrows

The pain endured after will be
Too unbearable and untold
Making a person to go insane
By hurting the mind manifold

— Raj

3. A happy life is all about

yq_restzone

A happy life is all about

A happy life is all about
Leading a carefree life
What ever be the payout
Love never fades away

A city built on pure love
Where hatred runs away
Enjoy freedom of desire
Where the divine soul say

— Raj

4. A lonely person knows

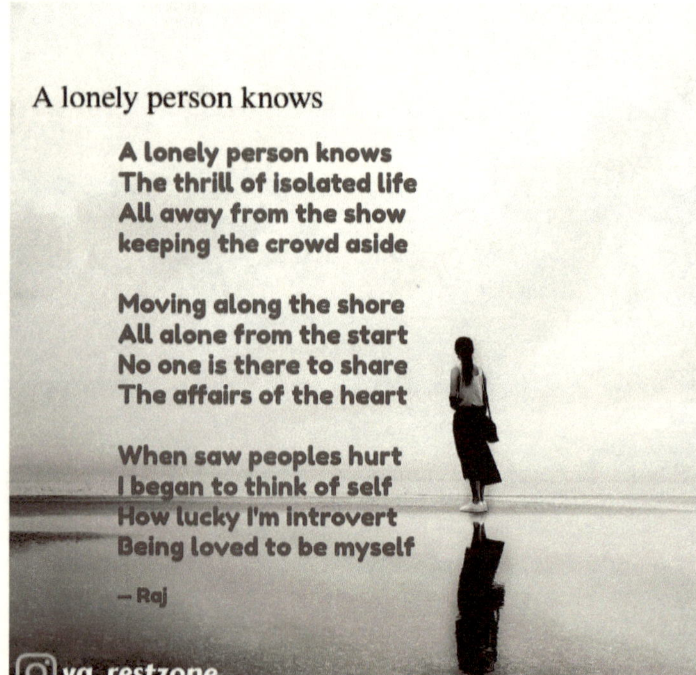

A lonely person knows

A lonely person knows
The thrill of isolated life
All away from the show
keeping the crowd aside

Moving along the shore
All alone from the start
No one is there to share
The affairs of the heart

When saw peoples hurt
I began to think of self
How lucky I'm introvert
Being loved to be myself

— Raj

yq_restzone

5. Although I like to wait

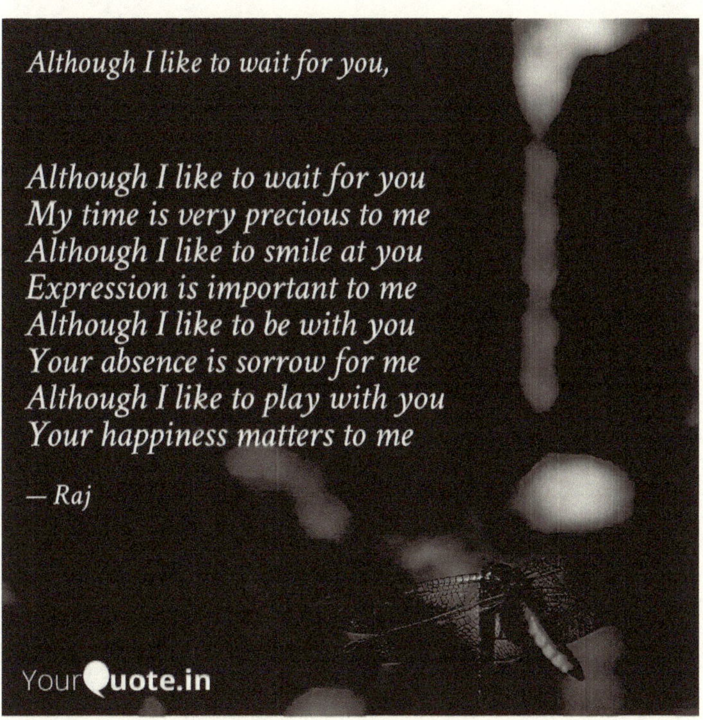

Although I like to wait for you,

Although I like to wait for you
My time is very precious to me
Although I like to smile at you
Expression is important to me
Although I like to be with you
Your absence is sorrow for me
Although I like to play with you
Your happiness matters to me

— Raj

YourQuote.in

6. Anger and love are

Anger and love are like

Anger and love are like
Two sides of the same coin
Where if love exists anger dissappears
And if anger exists love dissappears

— Raj

7. Beauty of the night

• 7 •

Beauty of the Night

The beauty of the night
Moon and stars at sight
Rivers reflecting the light
And it flows towards right

The noise soothes the mind
Breeze too cold and kind
Where darkness is so bind
Moonlight evades the blind

With no one on the street
Solitude feels like sweet
Blowing the mind in discreet
Soul's radiance is at its fleet

Sadness goes with beautiful smile
Moving along with flowing tide
Chillness soothes the heat inside
Happiness flowing full and wide

— Raj

8. Every story has

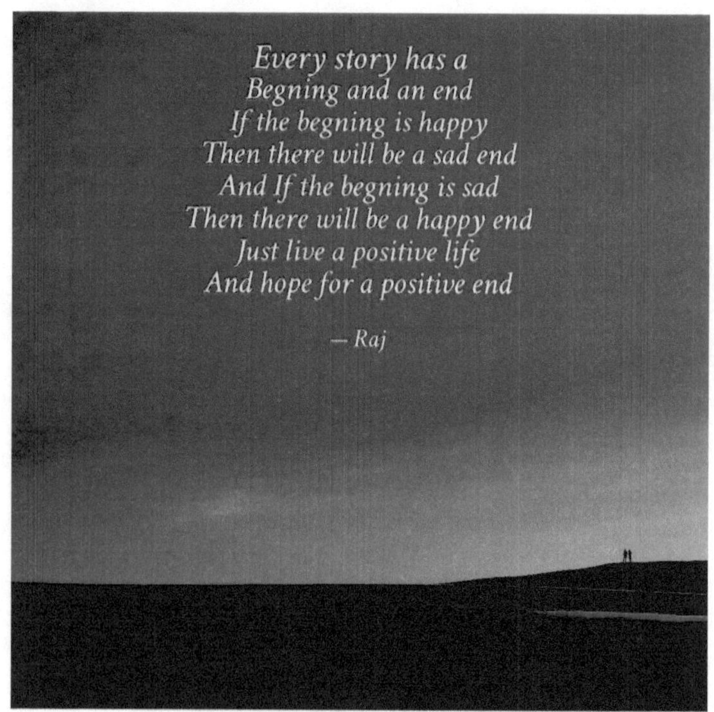

Every story has a
Begning and an end
If the begning is happy
Then there will be a sad end
And If the begning is sad
Then there will be a happy end
Just live a positive life
And hope for a positive end

— Raj

9. Books make it easier

Books make it easier

Books make it easier
To understand the basic
Essence of the knowledge
By reading the content's in it

— Raj

YourQuote.in

10. The change I'm longing for

The change I'm longing for

The change I'm longing for
Will happen after the war
Where there will be some lifes
That will exist eradicating the crowd
The world will become a place
Where it will be difficult to live
People that remains running here
Searching a place for them to heal

— Raj

11. Cherry

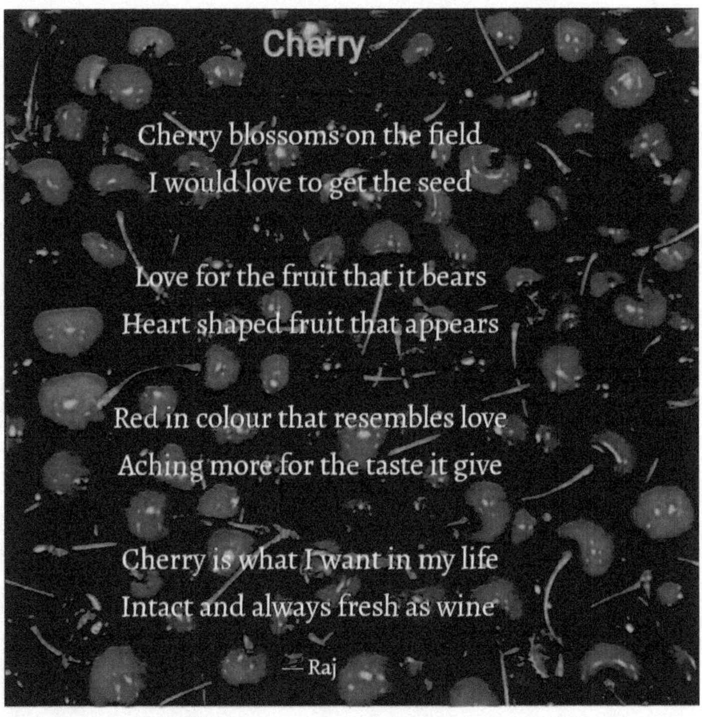

Cherry

Cherry blossoms on the field
I would love to get the seed

Love for the fruit that it bears
Heart shaped fruit that appears

Red in colour that resembles love
Aching more for the taste it give

Cherry is what I want in my life
Intact and always fresh as wine

— Raj

12. Comfort is that old friend

Comfort is that old friend

Comfort is that old friend
Which never let's you go
It stays there with you forever
And comes back like flamenco

– Raj

13. Countless

बेहिसाब / **Countless**

Countless people are running for life
While countless of them lost their lives

The aftermath of the war is disastrous
So stop the war and relieve the stress

— Raj

Rest Zone

14. Vampire's

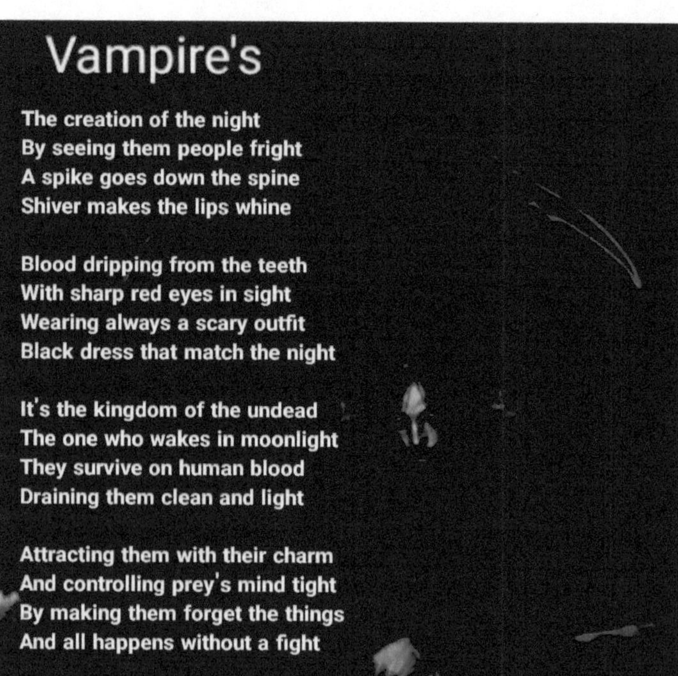

Vampire's

The creation of the night
By seeing them people fright
A spike goes down the spine
Shiver makes the lips whine

Blood dripping from the teeth
With sharp red eyes in sight
Wearing always a scary outfit
Black dress that match the night

It's the kingdom of the undead
The one who wakes in moonlight
They survive on human blood
Draining them clean and light

Attracting them with their charm
And controlling prey's mind tight
By making them forget the things
And all happens without a fight

— Raj

15. Darkness gives a message

Darkness gives a message
That dawn is very near
Move along with the light
There is no need to fear

Albeit darkness exists now
Brightness comes along with it
If the time is bad for you now
Goodness comes along with it

— Raj

16. Haunted

HAUNTED

Desolated citadel at a far away place
Where human beings never dare to pace
Paranormals labelled it as haunted place
Where dark nights and lightning strike

Whispers and hissing heard here and there
With howls and barks voicing the space
Where the stories of ghosts spread at dine
By hearing it a shiver runs down the spine

Impalpable impressions near the meadow
Where swift of wind suddenly starts to flow
Inside, in a hall where the fire place glow
Surrounded by silence and black cat meow

Curtains of windows starts to move to and fro
Breaking the silence the air begins to blow
Flicker of lights and a shadow seen and go
Increasing the fright and consciousness go

— Raj

17. Each time life hurts you

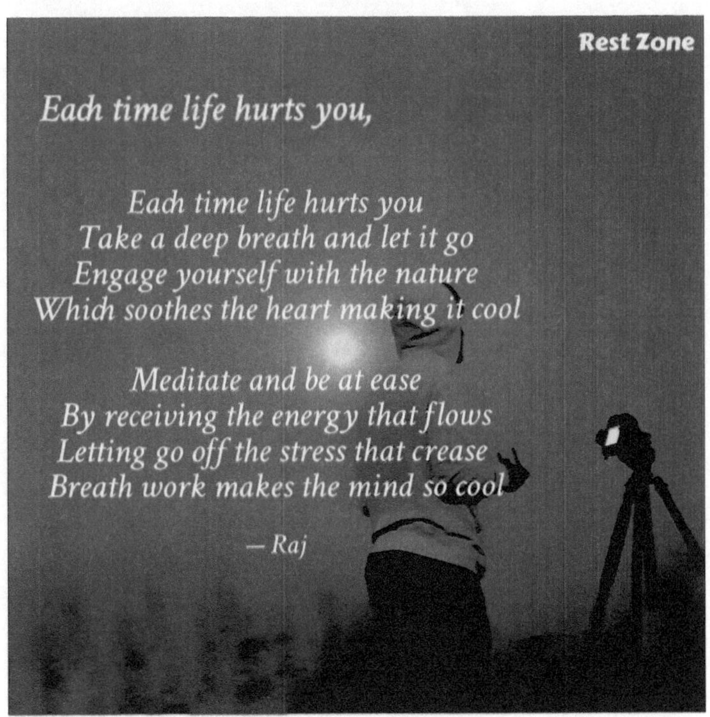

Rest Zone

Each time life hurts you,

Each time life hurts you
Take a deep breath and let it go
Engage yourself with the nature
Which soothes the heart making it cool

Meditate and be at ease
By receiving the energy that flows
Letting go off the stress that crease
Breath work makes the mind so cool

— Raj

18. Every night is a story

Every night is a story
That ends with dawn
The morning sunrise
Brings joy unknown

Day creates new path
For the story to be told
When night comes again
A new story gets unfold

— Raj

19. Every day is a journey

Every day is a journey

In the so-called book of life
Every day is a new chapter
Exploring the new that arrive
At dawn and sets there after

Every day is a journey here
That goes on throughout life
Paving a way that allows to fare
And to explore the life in rife

It goes on and on until the end
And makes us learn life's lesson
It gives time and allows to mend
The past mistakes by restoration

– Raj

20. Everyone is lost

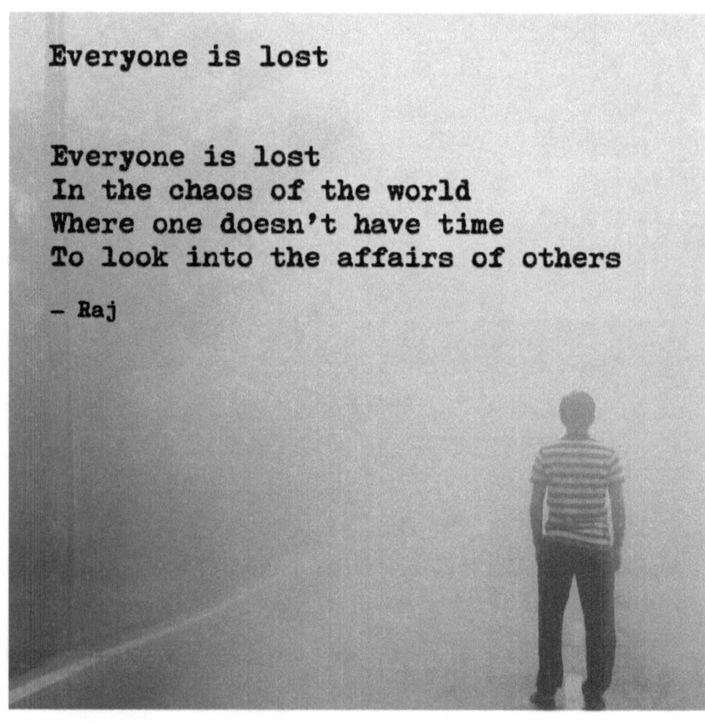

Everyone is lost

Everyone is lost
In the chaos of the world
Where one doesn't have time
To look into the affairs of others

- Raj

21. Every Poem I wrote for you

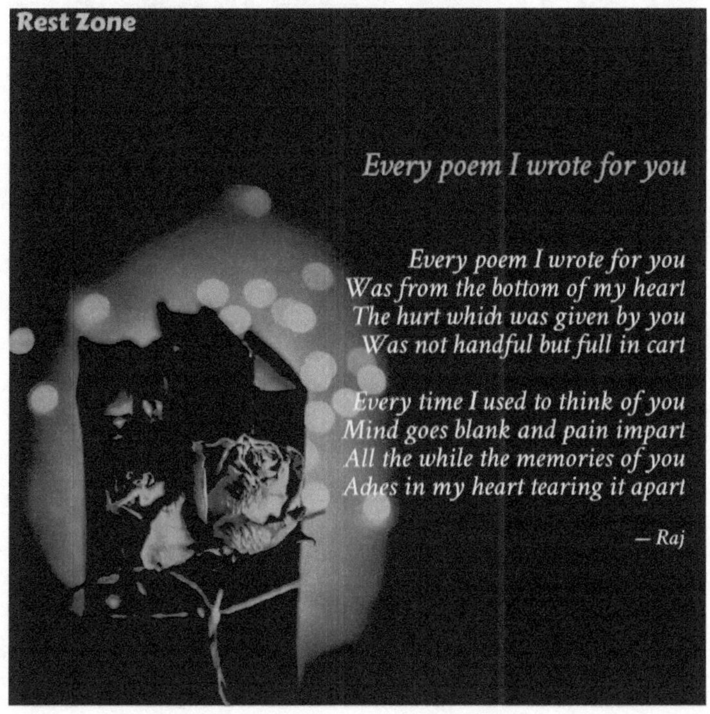

Rest Zone

Every poem I wrote for you

Every poem I wrote for you
Was from the bottom of my heart
The hurt which was given by you
Was not handful but full in cart

Every time I used to think of you
Mind goes blank and pain impart
All the while the memories of you
Aches in my heart tearing it apart

— Raj

22. Universe's Love

UNIVERSE'S LOVE

Everytime I think of you
My heart beats only for you
O my universe where are you
Come and let me to feel you

Let the chill go down my spine
Make me intoxicated like wine
Craving for love which is mine
I am waiting to feel the divine

Touch of you soothes my soul
Making me calm and powerful
Things which you gave plentiful
Thanks to you and am grateful

From birth till the time I depart
O my universe be in my heart
Let the energy flow in a spurt
Making me healthy and smart

— Raj

23. My days are all dark

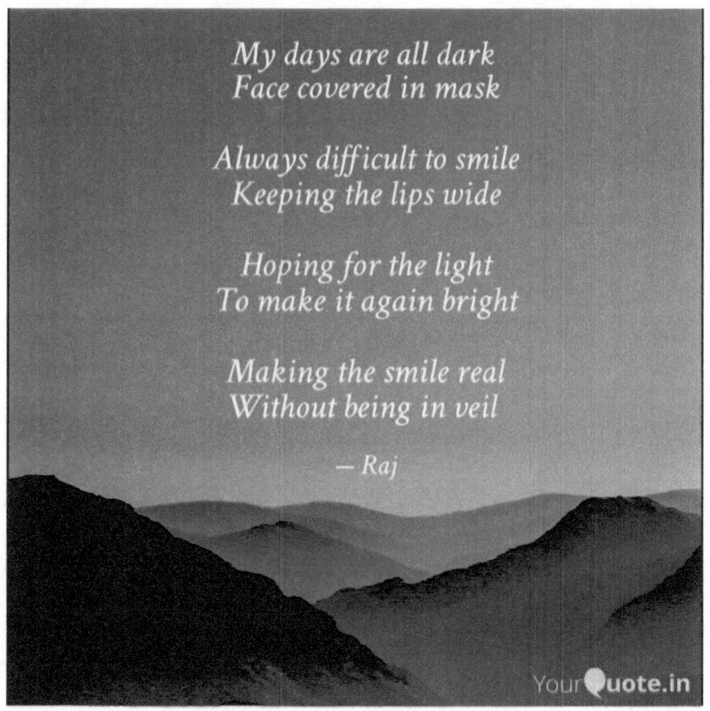

My days are all dark
Face covered in mask

Always difficult to smile
Keeping the lips wide

Hoping for the light
To make it again bright

Making the smile real
Without being in veil

— Raj

Your Quote.in

24. Fire and Ice are like

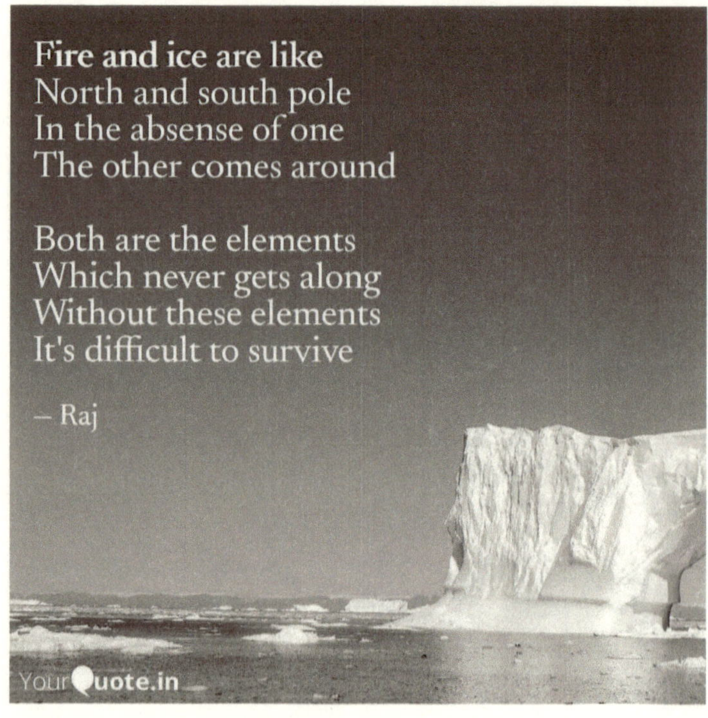
Fire and ice are like
North and south pole
In the absense of one
The other comes around

Both are the elements
Which never gets along
Without these elements
It's difficult to survive

– Raj

YourQuote.in

25. Past

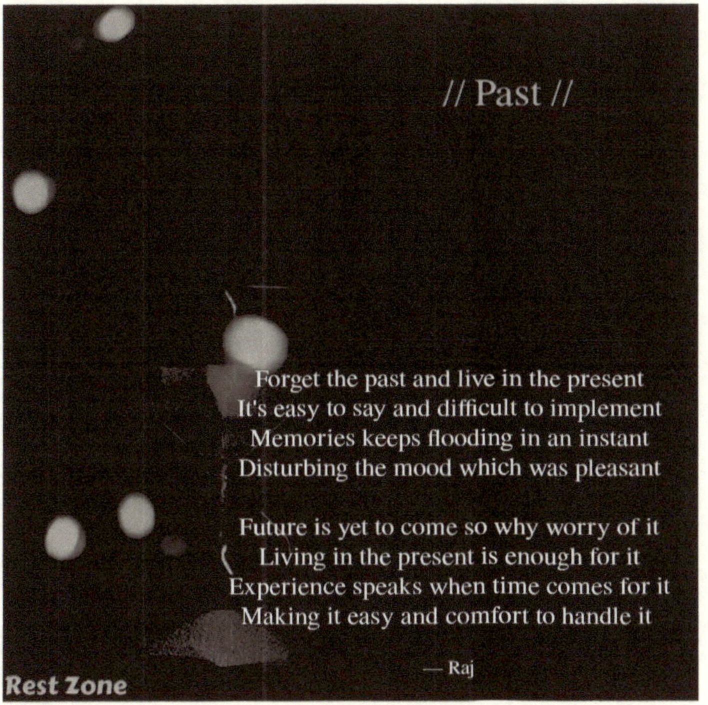

// Past //

Forget the past and live in the present
It's easy to say and difficult to implement
Memories keeps flooding in an instant
Disturbing the mood which was pleasant

Future is yet to come so why worry of it
Living in the present is enough for it
Experience speaks when time comes for it
Making it easy and comfort to handle it

— Raj

Rest Zone

26. The fragrance of rose

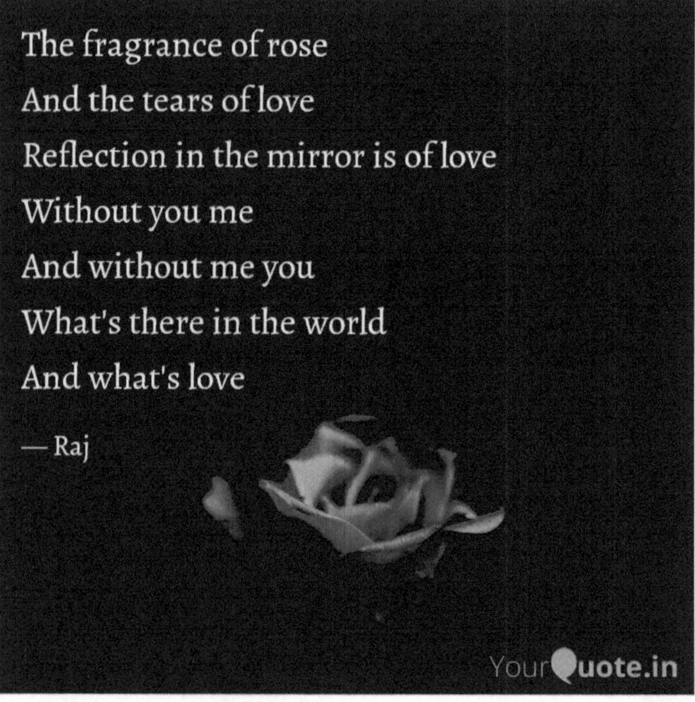
The fragrance of rose
And the tears of love
Reflection in the mirror is of love
Without you me
And without me you
What's there in the world
And what's love

—Raj

YourQuote.in

27. The heart knows

The heart knows
The pain and happiness
How much it crave
For the love selfless

The beauty of the heart
Is considered flawless
The pain it endures
Sometimes is endless

— Raj

28. The wounds in my heart

Rest Zone
The wounds in my heart

How much I try from the start
To heal the wounds in my heart
Now it has become my life's part
Will remain like that until I depart

— Raj

29. Nobody can heal

Nobody can heal
The hurt of the soul
As the time passes by
Lightens the pain
Endured

— Raj

30. In the poetry of life

In the poetry of life,
In the poetry of life
There are many strives
From sorrow to happiness
Everything feels like strife

If a loving heart is born
Hatred overcomes the love
Where the people are sworn
To break the heart and dive

Some moments are of the past
Where the pain usually resides
Some moments are the happiest
Which fills the heart like tides

Well, the cycle of life continues
Until the end of the cosmos
Where the sorrows are sung
With the beats of heart in chaos

– Raj

Rest Zone

31. Hellish World

• 31 •

Hellish World

It was just a matter of hours
Where the bad omen hovers

Making fool of the people well
Where over smartness dwell

Hurting the peoples sentiments
Abusing and laughing at times

Hatered and commotion wails
And where negativity prevails

Where power of the rich boom
Ostracizing poors is accustom

Mentality of people changed a lot
Maintaining all the levels to rot

This is not the world what I wish
Living here is painful and hellish

— Raj

32. Love is a drink

Love is a drink made up of
Juice extracted from sweet poison
It is a mixture of pleassure and pain
And has a lot of side effects
Unsatisfaction of this drink
Leaves the heart broken
Enduring a lot of pain
Where there is no medication

— Raj

33. Karma

Karma *is the sum of a persons good and bad actions in this life as well as past lives which is the cause and effects the future. Good Karma has good life and Bad Karma has bad life. It keeps on carrying forward until it gets nullified. As we say "reap the seed what you sow". In short it depends on the person's action.*

— Raj

34. It's going to be hard

It's going to be hard
To lead the life desired
Climbing the ladder
Of life and to get tired

To reach the destination
Without anymore hurdle
Is like a dream come true
Which is never possible

— Raj

35. The shade of love

Rest Zone
The shade of love
Let the shade of love begin to fall
Erase hatred from the heart of all

Make the cosmos a better place
And let the people begin to solace

— Raj
Sketch by - ARSH SINGH NAYAK

36. Life for dreamers is

Life for dreamers is

Life is a dream
Feels like ice cream

When it melts down
Makes you feel frown

Life for dreamers is
Like a fog that settles

During dawn when rays appears
With every dew drops on leaves

— Raj

37. What is life?

What is life?

Life is a game

Paly it without any shame

It's a mixture of happiness

and is followed by sadness

UP's and downs are a part

Playing with it is called an art

— Raj

38. Life seems incomplete

*Life seems incomplete
in the absence of*

*Life seems incomplete
In the absence of love
Will you be my Valentine
To sow the seeds of love*

*Let the seed spurt to plant
spread like never ending fire
Let it grow into a full tree
Spread it's branches worldwide*

— Raj

39. Some chapters

Some chapters

Life's Lessons is a book untold
With new chapter's to get unfold
Some chapters can not be told
Some happy moments many fold

A mixture of sadness and happiness
It's called life always with perfectness
Sometimes people feels it's vastness
Sometimes it's filled with sadness

— Raj

40. To end the darkness

• 40 •

To end the darkness called ignorance,
Light the brightness called experience

Learn to aquire what ever is possible
Increase the brightness by knowledge

— Raj

YourQuote.in

41. Like a bird, my heart

Like a bird, my heart

Like a bird, my heart
Aches to fly high in the sky
To explore the world so vast
And to reach the upper high

Flying from place to place
Sit on the branch so high
To build a home in the space
Where I can dwell without shy

To view the moon and the stars
To enjoy every beautiful sunrise
My heart aches to free the bars
And to flee, breaking all ties

— Raj

42. Like a broken leaf,

Rest Zone

Like a broken leaf,

In the journey of life
There comes a time
When time fades away
Old age comes to strive

It is like a broken leaf,
From a branch of a tree
With no one here to share
The pain and later die

— Raj

43. The life of a lonely person

The life of a lonely person
Is like a boat without a sailor
Thats free to roam around
Without any fixed direction
It keeps on sailing all alone
Without any hindrances
Unless and until it reaches
It's own final destination

— Raj

44. Loneliness

• 44 •

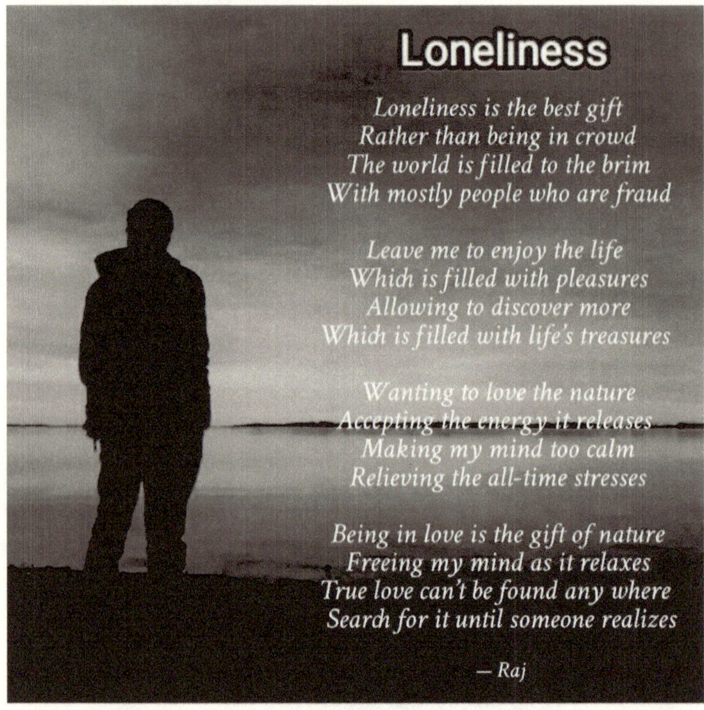

Loneliness

Loneliness is the best gift
Rather than being in crowd
The world is filled to the brim
With mostly people who are fraud

Leave me to enjoy the life
Which is filled with pleasures
Allowing to discover more
Which is filled with life's treasures

Wanting to love the nature
Accepting the energy it releases
Making my mind too calm
Relieving the all-time stresses

Being in love is the gift of nature
Freeing my mind as it relaxes
True love can't be found any where
Search for it until someone realizes

— Raj

45. Love is like music

Love is like music

Dancing to the tune
Listening to the lyrics
The love is like music
And that makes you sick

Once you get addicted
You can't live without it
And if file got corrupted
You become crazy for it

— Raj

46. Meditation isn't just

Meditation isn't just
Sitting with closed eyes
But if it is done properly
Will attain a lot of power

To awaken the dormant
Meditation helps a lot
By awakening the power
One reaches higher
consciousness

— *Raj*

YourQuote.in

47. Meditation leads us to

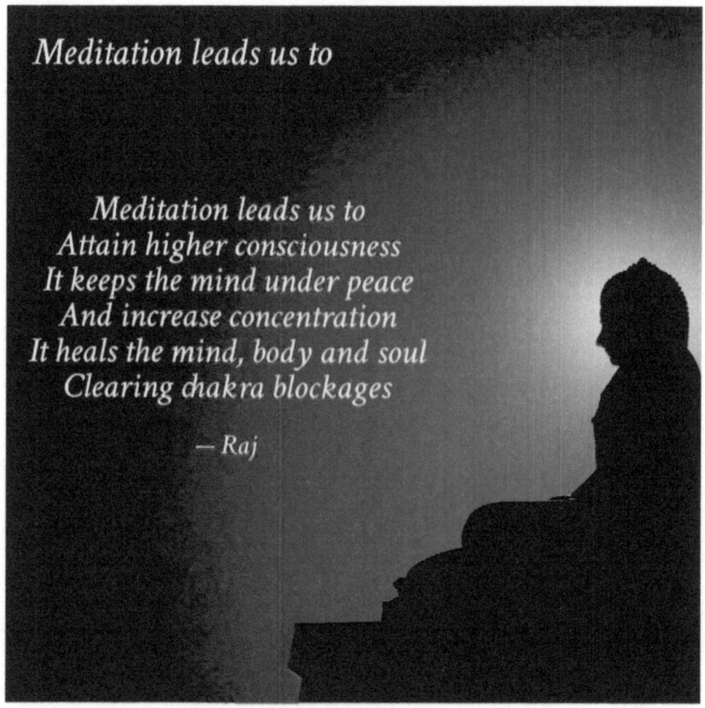

Meditation leads us to

Meditation leads us to
Attain higher consciousness
It keeps the mind under peace
And increase concentration
It heals the mind, body and soul
Clearing chakra blockages

— Raj

48. The morning takes away

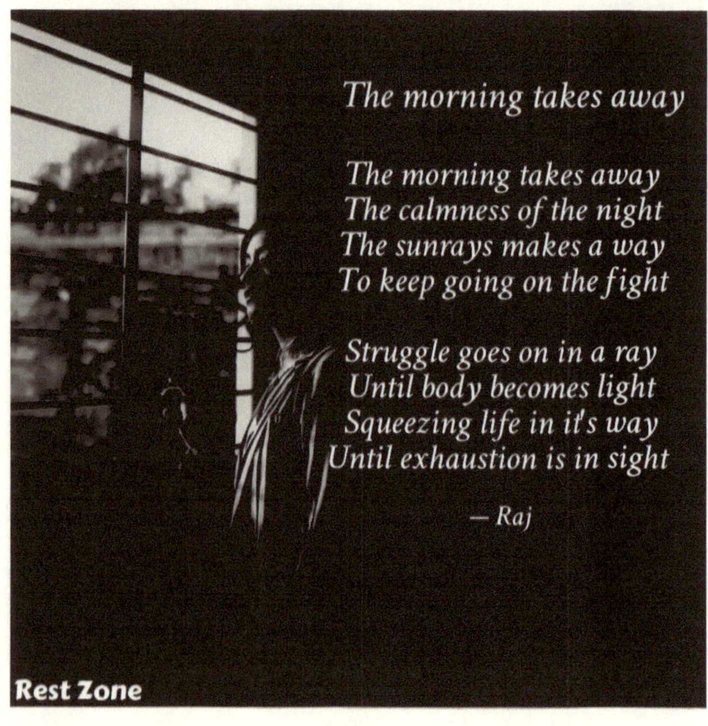

The morning takes away

The morning takes away
The calmness of the night
The sunrays makes a way
To keep going on the fight

Struggle goes on in a ray
Until body becomes light
Squeezing life in it's way
Until exhaustion is in sight

— Raj

Rest Zone

49. Paradise of my dreams

Paradise of my dreams

Mountain's seen in a straight line
River's flowing beneath like Tyne

A wooden castle and path sandy
Having a fire place with chimney

The place surrounded by the trees
As old as ever and the cold breeze

Enchanting the eyes and the mind
The landscape loving and so kind

Love that blooms from the heart
Longevity feeling from the start

Intermittent snow falls everywhere
Spreading like the blanket of white

Where songs of chirping birds heard
Melody soothing the nerves frayed

The valley sweetness flows in streams
And that's the paradise of my dreams

— Raj

50. My heart is an ocean

My heart is an ocean

My heart is an ocean
Filled with full of emotion
Where love flows in a motion
To love God's lovely creation

The waves are in inclination
To reach the shore in fashion
Where people feels connection
With full of love and affection

— Raj

51. Everytime you smile

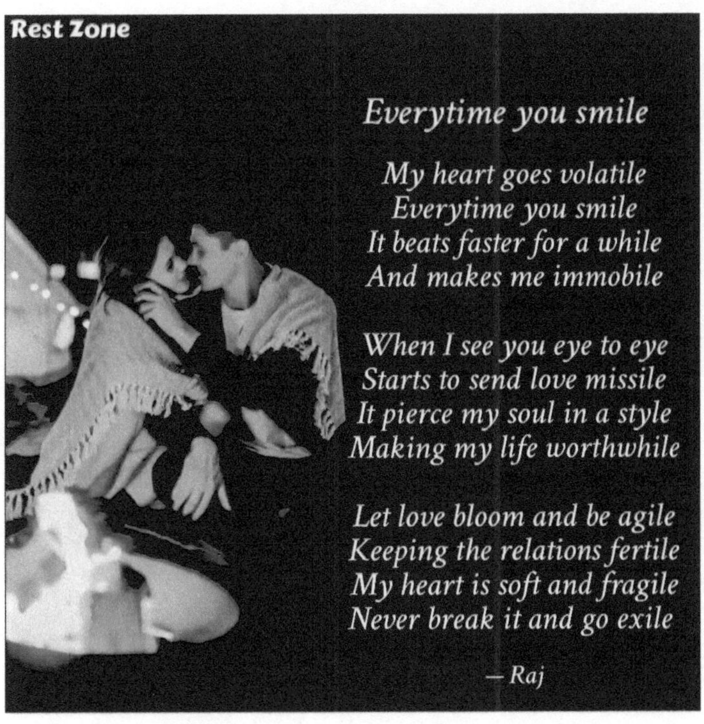

Everytime you smile

My heart goes volatile
Everytime you smile
It beats faster for a while
And makes me immobile

When I see you eye to eye
Starts to send love missile
It pierce my soul in a style
Making my life worthwhile

Let love bloom and be agile
Keeping the relations fertile
My heart is soft and fragile
Never break it and go exile

— Raj

52. No one understands

Rest Zone

No one understands

From night till the dawn
And from dawn till night
Why the sun raise and set?
Here no one understands

In a garden full of flowers
And being the queen of love
Why the rose rest on thorns?
Here no one understands

Leading a life in full harmony
Where love ceases to exist
Why there is pain in the heart?
Here no one understands

From the birth till the death
Mystery behind life and death
Why death comes after life?
Here no one understands

— Raj

53. Nobody can break

Nobody can break

Nobody can break the law of nature
If tried can get you on to a stretcher

Nobody can play with it's resources
If tried won't get back without wretches

It's the law of the nature

— Raj

54. Nobody knows how broken

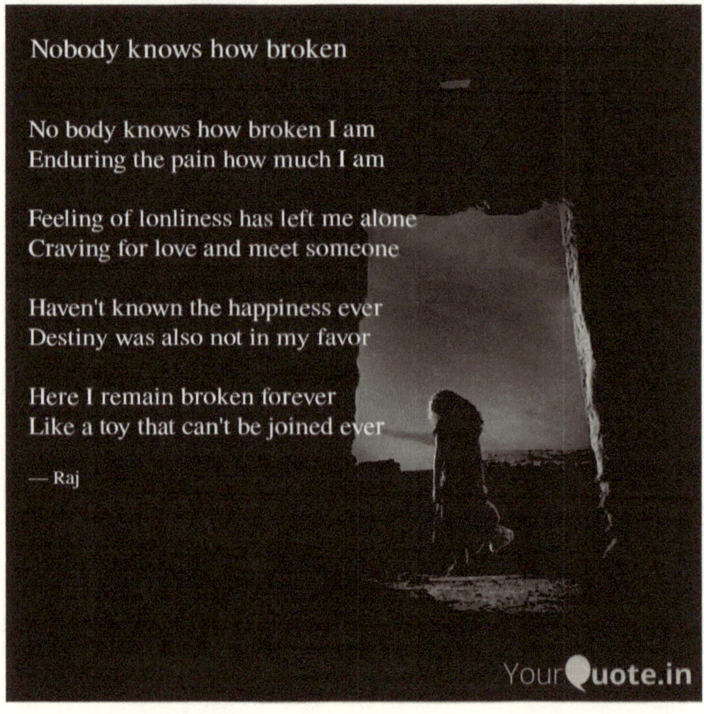

Nobody knows how broken

No body knows how broken I am
Enduring the pain how much I am

Feeling of lonliness has left me alone
Craving for love and meet someone

Haven't known the happiness ever
Destiny was also not in my favor

Here I remain broken forever
Like a toy that can't be joined ever

—Raj

YourQuote.in

55. Not every chapter in life

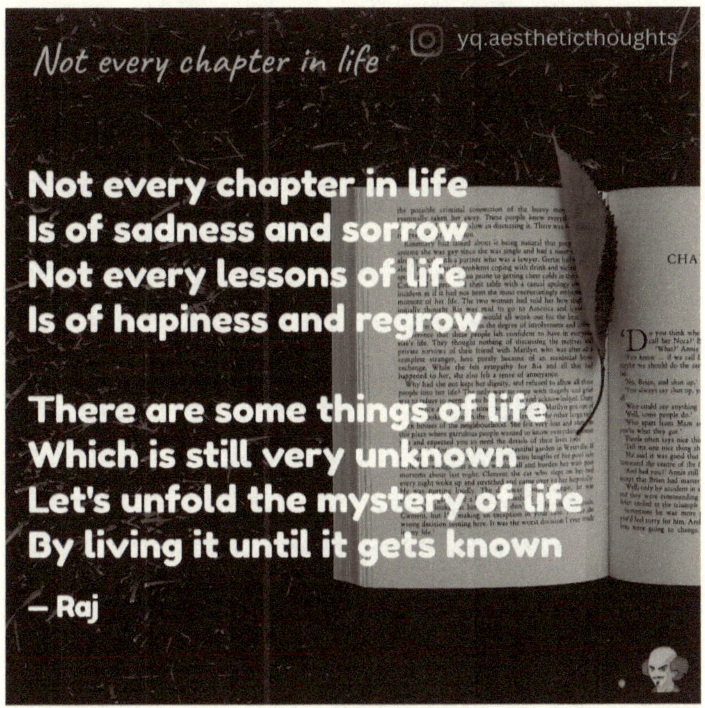
Not every chapter in life
yq.aestheticthoughts
Not every chapter in life
Is of sadness and sorrow
Not every lessons of life
Is of hapiness and regrow

There are some things of life
Which is still very unknown
Let's unfold the mystery of life
By living it until it gets known

— Raj

56. The beauty we seek

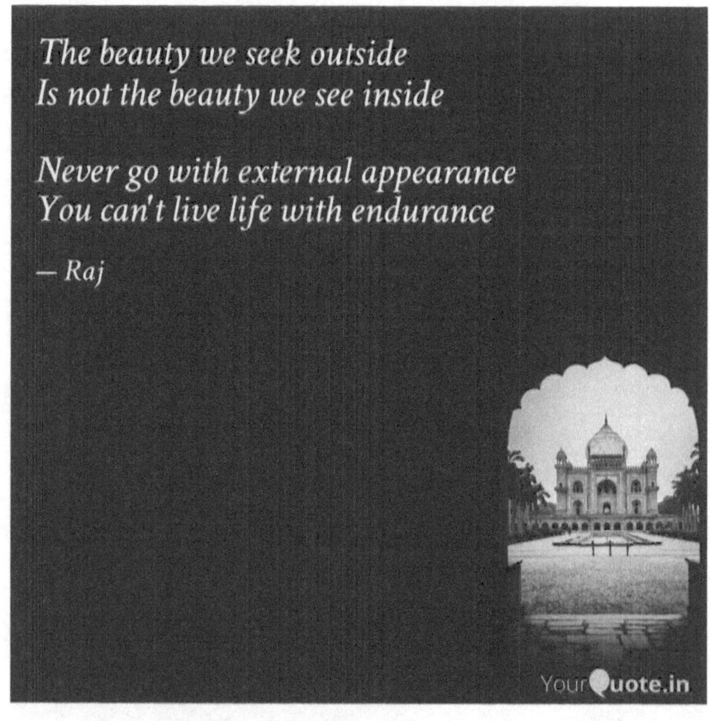

The beauty we seek outside
Is not the beauty we see inside

Never go with external appearance
You can't live life with endurance

— Raj

57. Our lives are as...

Our lives are as unpredictable as

Our lives are as unpredictable as the climate
It keeps on changing depending on time and date

It's how we nourish and cherish the ongoing life
Depending on serendipity more than desire

— Raj

58. In the pages of your heart

In the pages of your heart

In the pages of your heart
I wish to store my painting
So that you can be a part
And always keep adoring

Let's take part in a concert
And keep ourselves singing
The melody of love and art
Bloom in and start dancing

— Raj

Rest Zone

59. People are like clothes

People are like clothes

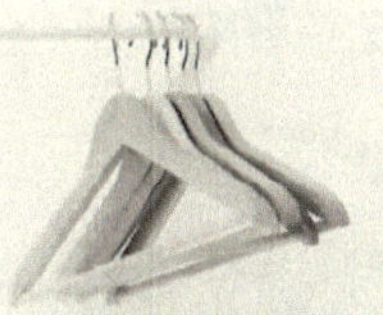

Wandering around the world
I met with a variety of people
Some young and some are old
With antique tastes and culture

Some were too cozy and warm
Always displaying smile and charm
Some were hostile and unwelcome
Giving pain to the ones who come

As far as goes my examination
I Felt people are like clothes
They tend to change very often
Like their minds are in chaos

— Raj

60. People hurt you if

Rest Zone

People hurt you if

People hurt you if
You are lenient and loving
People hurt you if
You love them unconditionally
People hurt you if
You are kind and soft at heart
People hurt you if
You don't react to their scraps

– Raj

61. If plants could talk,

If plants could talk, they would say:
Don't destroy me, I give you shade

If you cut me down, it gives me pain
Give me a new birth by planting again

— Raj

YourQuote.in

62. As the sun moves away

Quotes for the Day

As the sun moves away creating a space for the moon
and the moon does the same
As the day moves away creating a space for the night
and the night does the same
Likewise is the life of humans in the universe

— Raj

Rest Zone

63. If you build a bridge

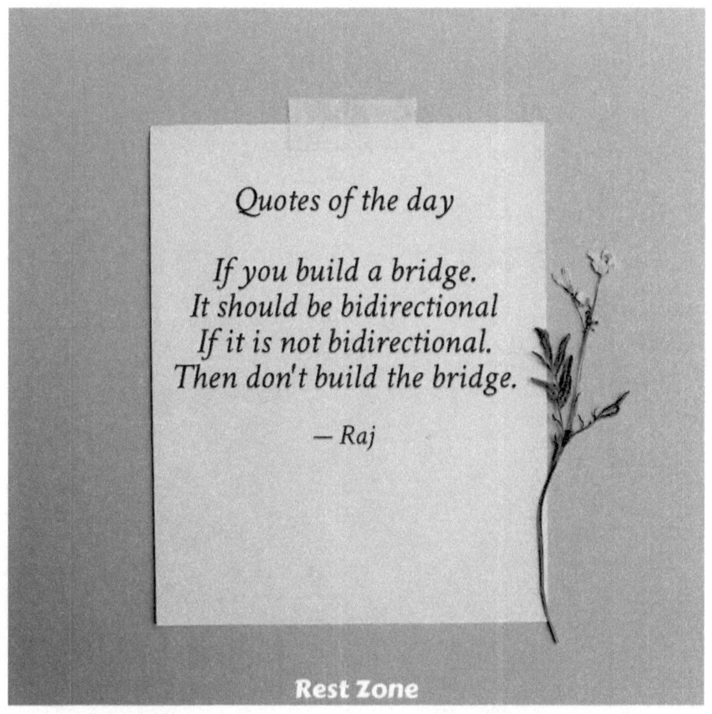

Quotes of the day

If you build a bridge.
It should be bidirectional
If it is not bidirectional.
Then don't build the bridge.

— Raj

Rest Zone

64. The real meaning of love

The real meaning of love is

The real meaning of love is
Unknown to many
Some live their life selfless
Thinking unconditionally
While some live being selfish
Receiving it so many

— Raj

Rest Zone

65. The reflection in the mirror

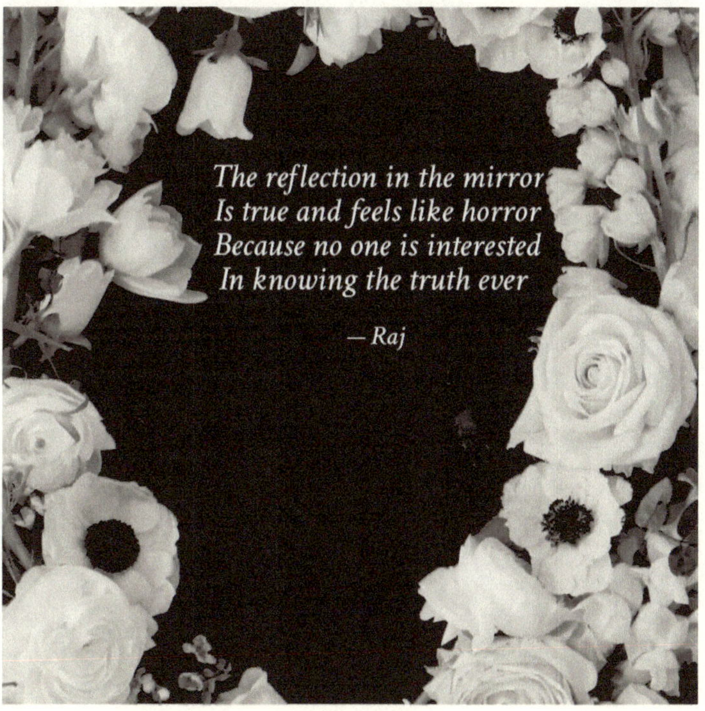

The reflection in the mirror
Is true and feels like horror
Because no one is interested
In knowing the truth ever

— Raj

66. The days of my past

The days of my past
Reminds me very vast
The days those we spent
In harmony with natures scent

— Raj

67. Some stories die

• 67 •

Some stories die

Some stories die while some survive
Not all stories are permanent or reprieve
Some are boring while some interesting
Stories that die always goes away missing

— Raj

68. In the state of loneliness

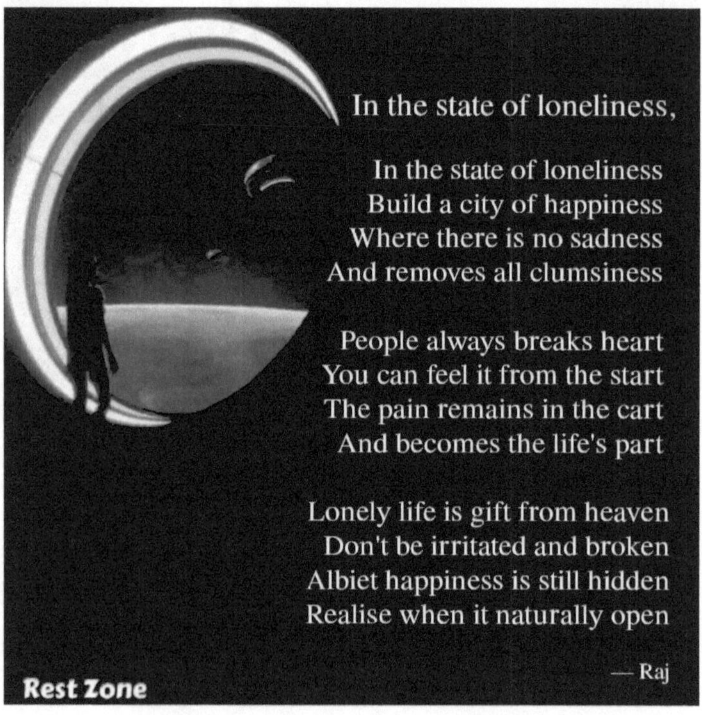

In the state of loneliness,

In the state of loneliness
Build a city of happiness
Where there is no sadness
And removes all clumsiness

People always breaks heart
You can feel it from the start
The pain remains in the cart
And becomes the life's part

Lonely life is gift from heaven
Don't be irritated and broken
Albiet happiness is still hidden
Realise when it naturally open

— Raj

Rest Zone

69. Mystic Nights

As the sun goes down and darkness creep
At midnight when all the people sleep

When profound silence reigns everywhere
And the mist seen slowly forming somewhere

Gusts of wind suddenly starts blowing
Tossing the fallen dried leaves as if whispering

The cries of babies is sometimes heard
Mingled eerily with howls of wolves from the sward

So mystic is the night and a scary sight
With silhouette moving around igniting fright

The scene chills up the bone and the nerve
If someone ever walks up through the curve

Mystical creatures appears in new moon night
While some can see it others just sense it right

The spirits of the dead coming from abyss
And the noise which can be heard in hiss

Where science can never claim to understand
Magical happenings of a new moon night still astound

Where witches and black magicians do their rituals
Dressing their part in scary outfits and skulls

Snaring the innocent and gullible people around
By feeding on their superstition in ample and sound

– Raj

Mystic Nights

70. Sunrise is a blessing

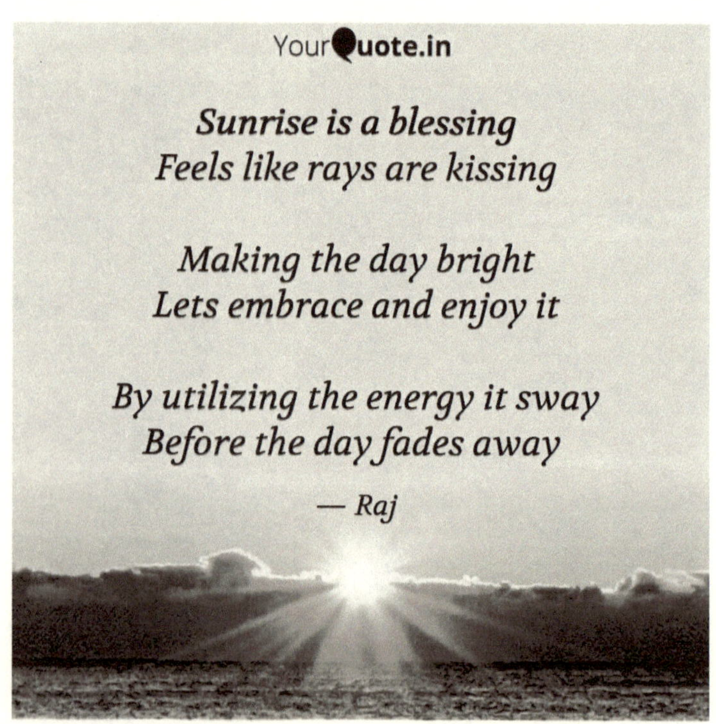
YourQuote.in
Sunrise is a blessing
Feels like rays are kissing

Making the day bright
Lets embrace and enjoy it

By utilizing the energy it sway
Before the day fades away

— Raj

71. Nothing is more valuable

Nothing is more valuable
Than the scene which we see
Nature has it's own value
Nothing can replace it

Life and soul are also valuable
But most of them doesn't see
People tends to buy everything
But money can't buy all that we see

— Raj

72. The journey of life

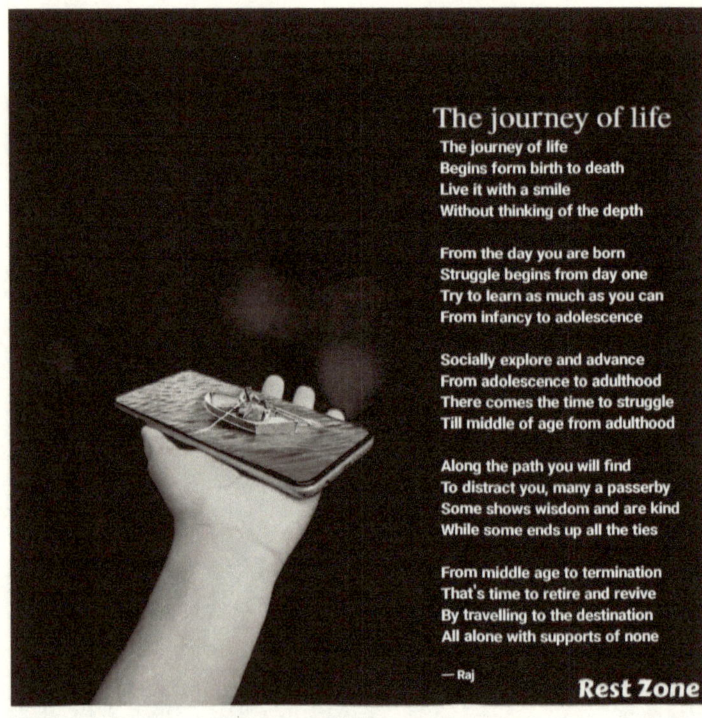

The journey of life
The journey of life
Begins form birth to death
Live it with a smile
Without thinking of the depth

From the day you are born
Struggle begins from day one
Try to learn as much as you can
From infancy to adolescence

Socially explore and advance
From adolescence to adulthood
There comes the time to struggle
Till middle of age from adulthood

Along the path you will find
To distract you, many a passerby
Some shows wisdom and are kind
While some ends up all the ties

From middle age to termination
That's time to retire and revive
By travelling to the destination
All alone with supports of none

— Raj

Rest Zone

73. The peace of midnight

The peace of midnight

The peace of midnight
Won't get in bright light
Where the world is crowded
With almost people half dead

Chaos spreaded everywhere
Where clamness is never felt
Night plays a magical game
Where most people are slept

— Raj

Rest Zone

74. Behind every broken heart

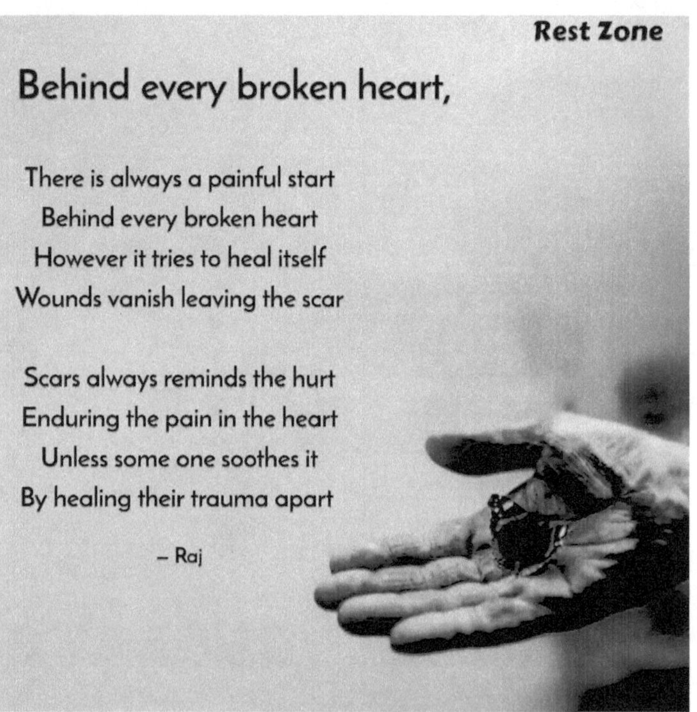

Rest Zone

Behind every broken heart,

There is always a painful start
Behind every broken heart
However it tries to heal itself
Wounds vanish leaving the scar

Scars always reminds the hurt
Enduring the pain in the heart
Unless some one soothes it
By healing their trauma apart

– Raj

75. Cross Road

Cross Road

There comes always a cross road in life
Where you are alone and have to decide
The path which leads to your destination
With out any fear and firm determination
Don't pay heed to people who criticize
Let your success make the noise...

— Raj

76. Behind every happy person

Behind every happy person
There is a sadness behind a veil
Although if it is not shown
It remains everytime with a seal

Wearing a smiling mask everytime
The person moves on with his life
Even though sadness stays all time
The person tries to hide it in rife

— Raj

:)

77. There's a thing about rain

There's a thing about rain

There's a thing about rain
Not even a drop goes in vain

Makes mind and the earth cool
Washing the crust making pool

— Raj

78. My wounds are a home to

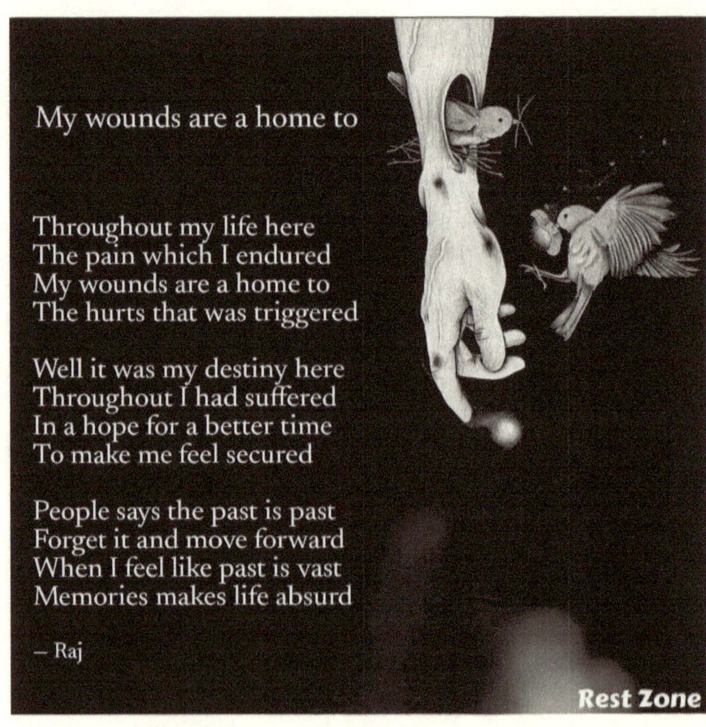

My wounds are a home to

Throughout my life here
The pain which I endured
My wounds are a home to
The hurts that was triggered

Well it was my destiny here
Throughout I had suffered
In a hope for a better time
To make me feel secured

People says the past is past
Forget it and move forward
When I feel like past is vast
Memories makes life absurd

— Raj

Rest Zone

79. In the cocoon of love

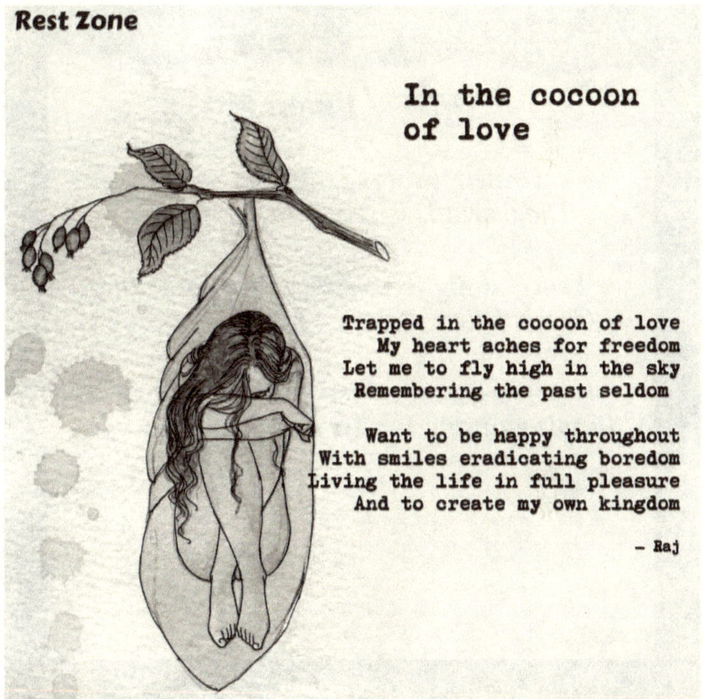

Rest Zone

In the cocoon
of love

Trapped in the cocoon of love
My heart aches for freedom
Let me to fly high in the sky
Remembering the past seldom

Want to be happy throughout
With smiles eradicating boredom
Living the life in full pleasure
And to create my own kingdom

— Raj

80. Union

युक्ति / Union

United we stand, divided we fall
The world is looking for union so far

Peaceful nights and days are not found
Chao's filled in the air and is all around

Hatered is everywhere without any gain
People running for life and is in lot of pain

— Raj

Rest Zone

81. Vagabond

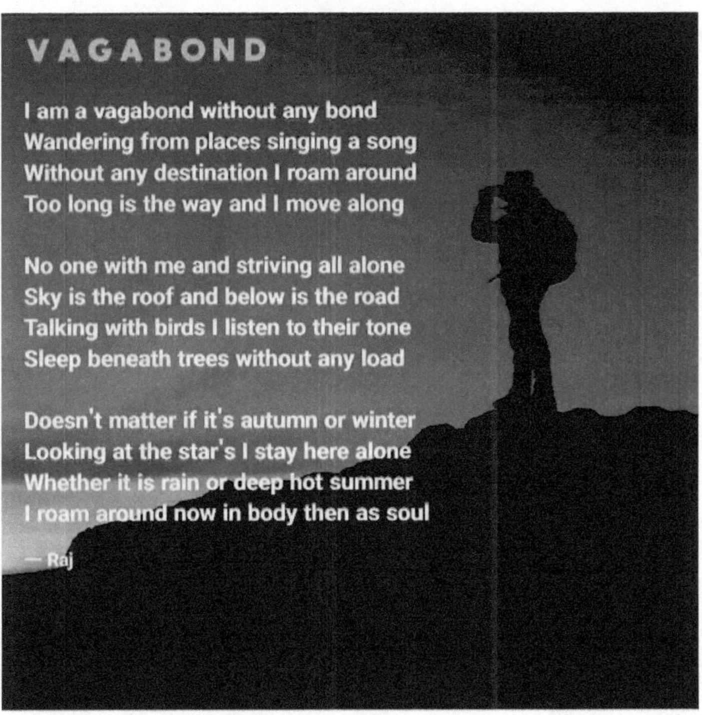

VAGABOND

I am a vagabond without any bond
Wandering from places singing a song
Without any destination I roam around
Too long is the way and I move along

No one with me and striving all alone
Sky is the roof and below is the road
Talking with birds I listen to their tone
Sleep beneath trees without any load

Doesn't matter if it's autumn or winter
Looking at the star's I stay here alone
Whether it is rain or deep hot summer
I roam around now in body then as soul

— Raj

82. Walk in the moon light

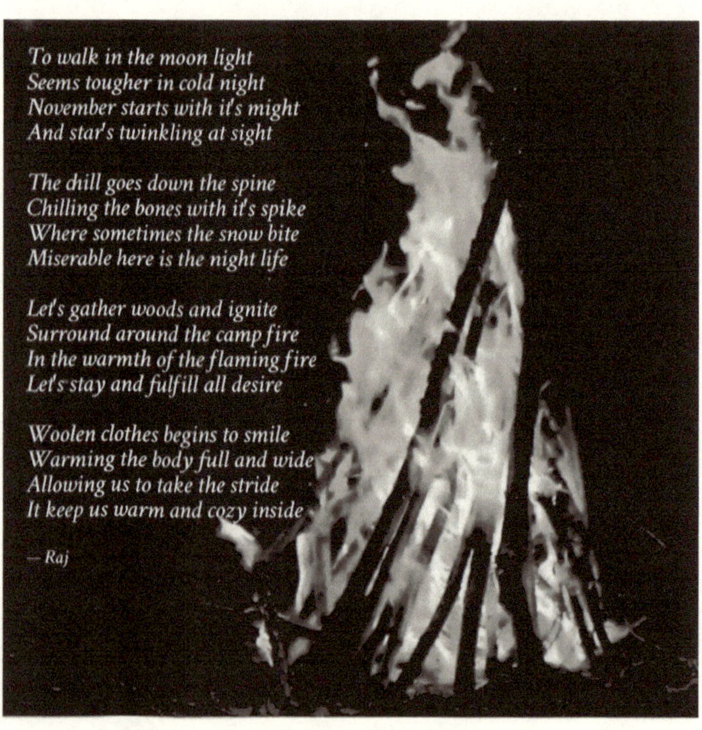

To walk in the moon light
Seems tougher in cold night
November starts with it's might
And star's twinkling at sight

The chill goes down the spine
Chilling the bones with it's spike
Where sometimes the snow bite
Miserable here is the night life

Let's gather woods and ignite
Surround around the camp fire
In the warmth of the flaming fire
Let's stay and fulfill all desire

Woolen clothes begins to smile
Warming the body full and wide
Allowing us to take the stride
It keep us warm and cozy inside

— Raj

83. War and Aftermath

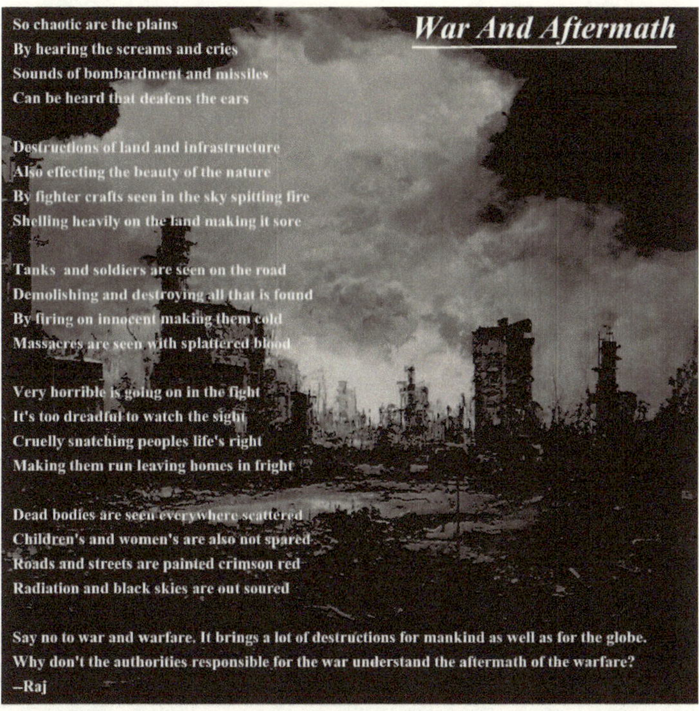

War And Aftermath

So chaotic are the plains
By hearing the screams and cries
Sounds of bombardment and missiles
Can be heard that deafens the ears

Destructions of land and infrastructure
Also effecting the beauty of the nature
By fighter crafts seen in the sky spitting fire
Shelling heavily on the land making it sore

Tanks and soldiers are seen on the road
Demolishing and destroying all that is found
By firing on innocent making them cold
Massacres are seen with splattered blood

Very horrible is going on in the fight
It's too dreadful to watch the sight
Cruelly snatching peoples life's right
Making them run leaving homes in fright

Dead bodies are seen everywhere scattered
Children's and women's are also not spared
Roads and streets are painted crimson red
Radiation and black skies are out soured

Say no to war and warfare. It brings a lot of destructions for mankind as well as for the globe.
Why don't the authorities responsible for the war understand the aftermath of the warfare?
—Raj

84. The warmth of your love

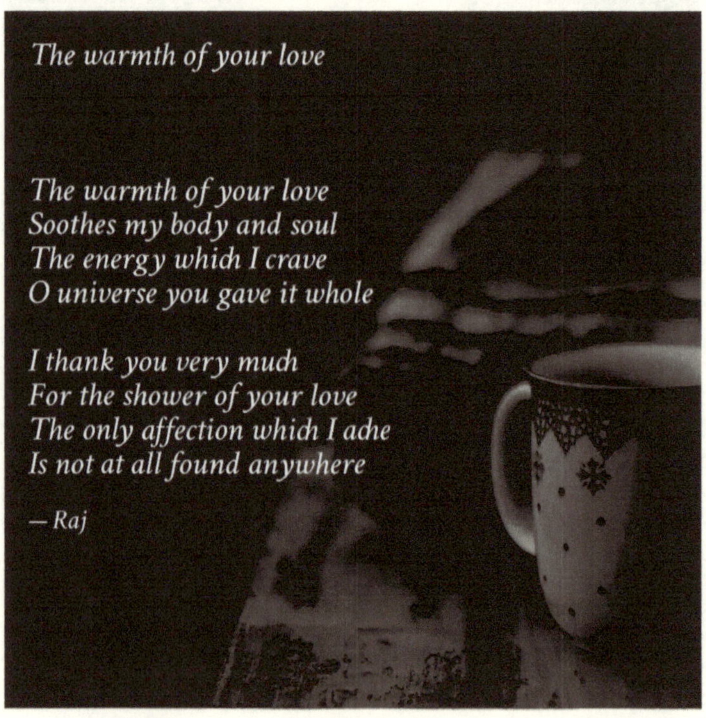

The warmth of your love

The warmth of your love
Soothes my body and soul
The energy which I crave
O universe you gave it whole

I thank you very much
For the shower of your love
The only affection which I ache
Is not at all found anywhere

—Raj

85. War can never be...

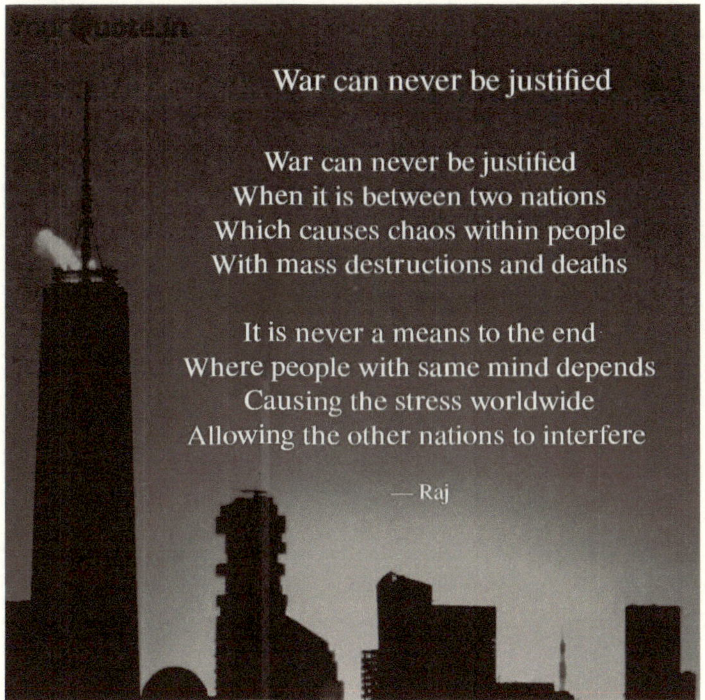
War can never be justified

War can never be justified
When it is between two nations
Which causes chaos within people
With mass destructions and deaths

It is never a means to the end
Where people with same mind depends
Causing the stress worldwide
Allowing the other nations to interfere

— Raj

86. Wasting time is like

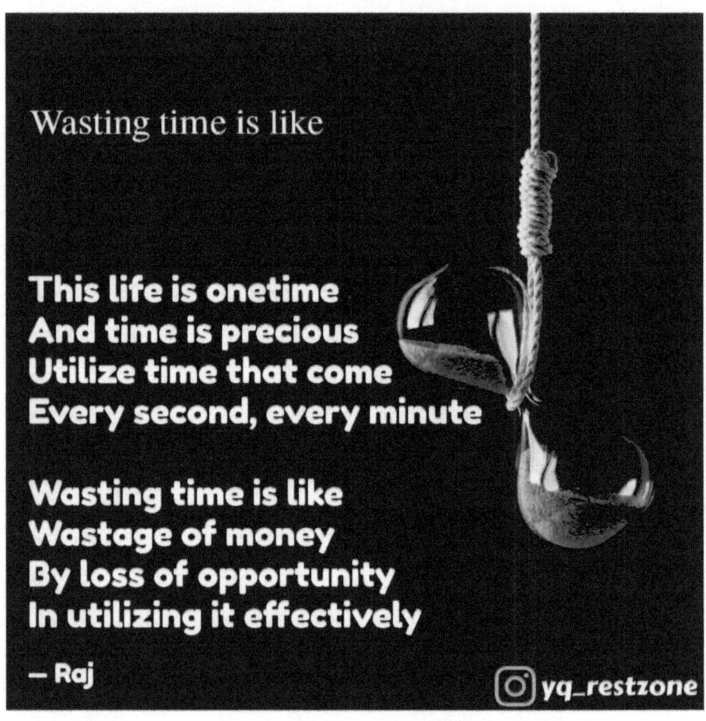

Wasting time is like

This life is onetime
And time is precious
Utilize time that come
Every second, every minute

Wasting time is like
Wastage of money
By loss of opportunity
In utilizing it effectively

— Raj

yq_restzone

87. What is true love?

yq.aestheticthoughts

What is true love?

Troughout the universe
Wandered from place to place
In search of the true love
But can not find anywhere

Everything is put on sale
And come with a price tag
Love is measured here
By looking at your status tag

True love means the love
Where body, mind and soul
Aligns with person you love
Without seeing the status quo

— Raj

88. Solitude

#NaPoWriMo29

~ Solitude ~

When ever there remains time
You are left sound and lone
People surrounds in happy time
And in grief they leave you alone

In your gain they really relishes
In your loss they shows their backs
In your laughs they merrily laughs
And if you cry no one really cares

You have relations if you are glad
They leave the moment you are sad
People persuade when you are good
They dissuade when situation is bad

Most of the time you are so alone
Enjoying the loneliness to the core
Away from the world and people
Calm and quiet living life in solitude

— Raj

Rest Zone

89. When I feel lonely

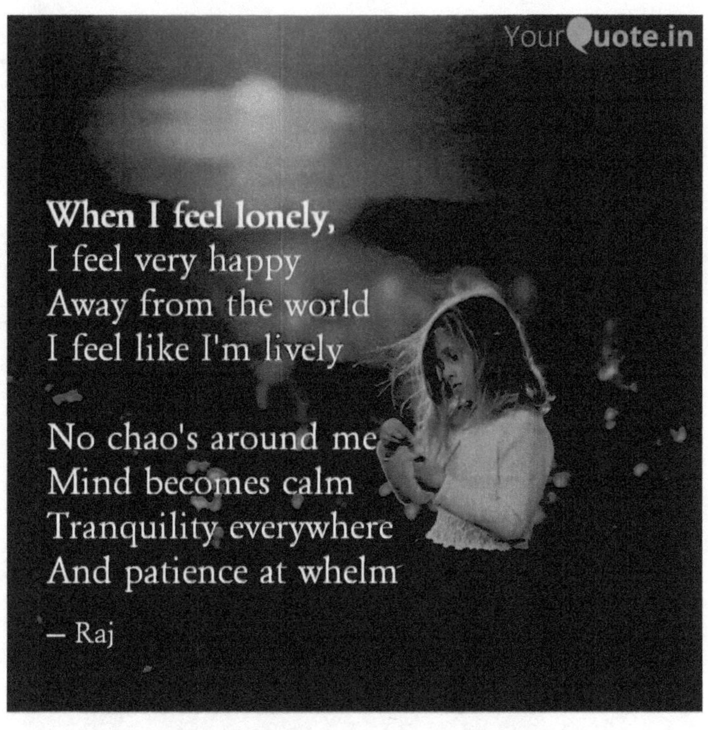

YourQuote.in
When I feel lonely,
I feel very happy
Away from the world
I feel like I'm lively

No chao's around me
Mind becomes calm
Tranquility everywhere
And patience at whelm

— Raj

90. When it's time to say goodbye

When it's time to say goodbye,

When it's time to say goodbye,
There's no much time left to buy
People gathered will start to cry
Until every fallen drops get's dry

People eager to fulfill last desire
Disposal of the corpse to the fire
Emotions welled up around pier
Until culmination and they retire

— Raj

91. When you feel like giving up

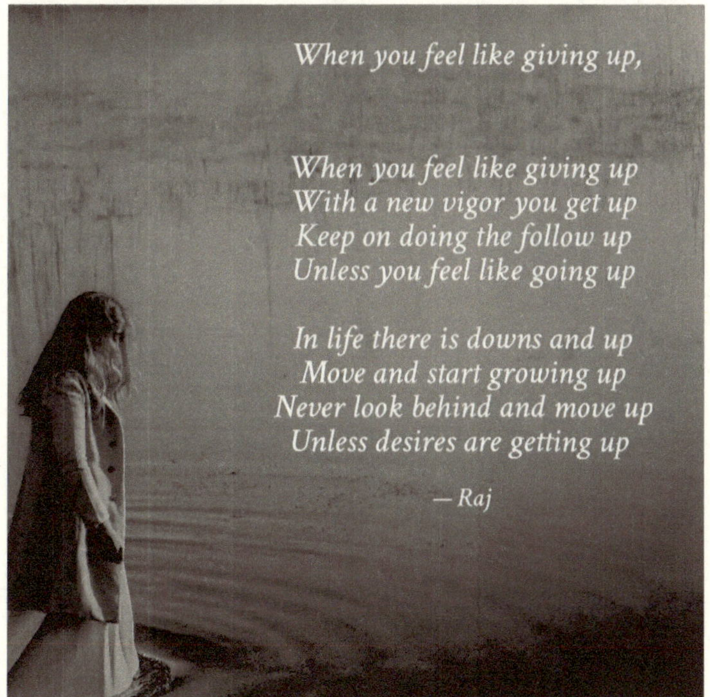

When you feel like giving up,

When you feel like giving up
With a new vigor you get up
Keep on doing the follow up
Unless you feel like going up

In life there is downs and up
Move and start growing up
Never look behind and move up
Unless desires are getting up

— Raj

92. When you get shattered

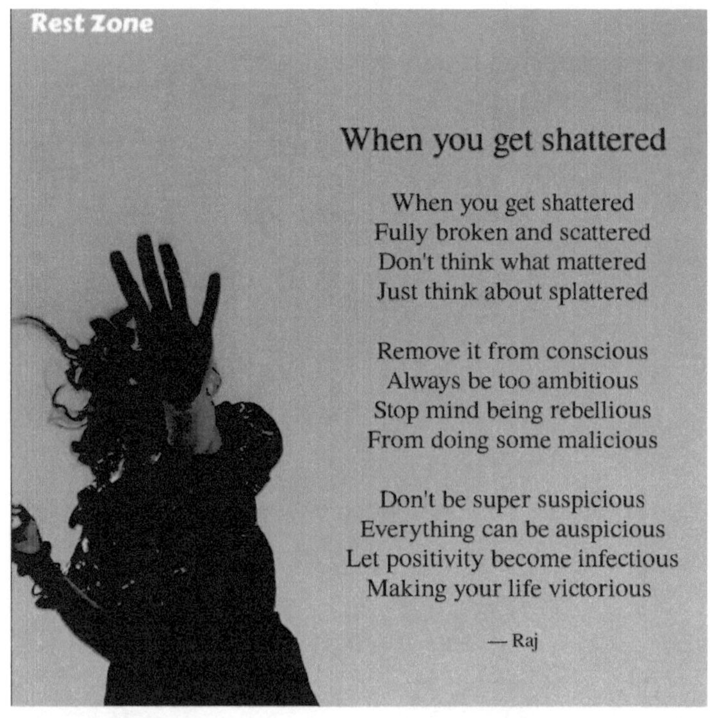

When you get shattered

When you get shattered
Fully broken and scattered
Don't think what mattered
Just think about splattered

Remove it from conscious
Always be too ambitious
Stop mind being rebellious
From doing some malicious

Don't be super suspicious
Everything can be auspicious
Let positivity become infectious
Making your life victorious

— Raj

93. Where the day ends

Where the day ends,

Where the day ends,
All tired and exhausted
The night begins to send
Signal to get invigorated

Fully energized at dawn
For a new day to begin
This goes without a mown
Until cycle repeats again

Well, this is life until the end
Daily it repeats again and again
Without a chance to transcend
Until life ends without any gain

– Raj

94. One thought that scares me

One thought that scares me the most
Whether the war will stop at any cost
After all the lifes what will remain the most
Only barren land which is filled with the ghost

With the radiation spread everywhere
Dead bodies found decayed somewhere
With Pungent smell spread everywhere
Making the remaining people run elsewhere

— Raj

95. The world isn't good for

The world isn't good for
People like me and you
Where people strive for
The eternal peace at fou

In a world like this where
The tranquility is at stake
Tell me o dear is there
Someone to cut the cake

— Raj

96. The world is missing

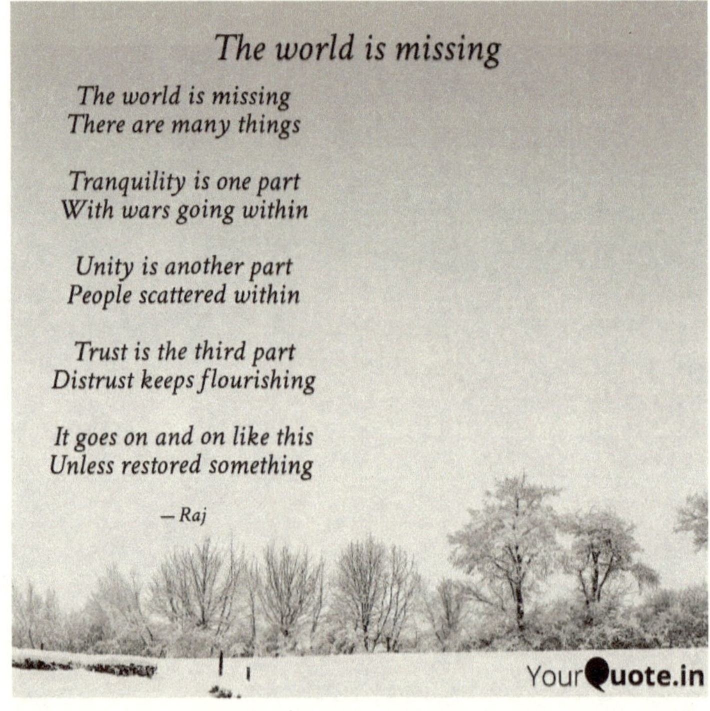

The world is missing

The world is missing
There are many things

Tranquility is one part
With wars going within

Unity is another part
People scattered within

Trust is the third part
Distrust keeps flourishing

It goes on and on like this
Unless restored something

— Raj

YourQuote.in

97. Wrath of nature

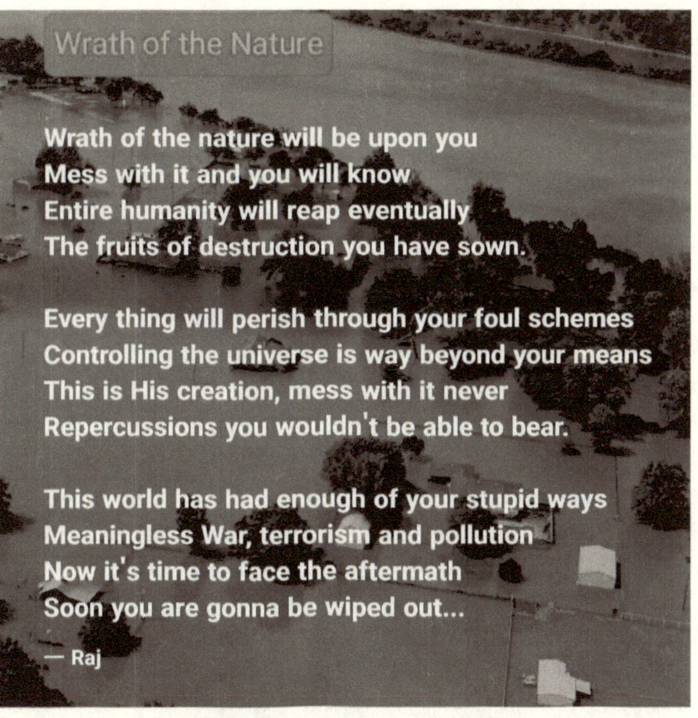

Wrath of the Nature

Wrath of the nature will be upon you
Mess with it and you will know
Entire humanity will reap eventually
The fruits of destruction you have sown.

Every thing will perish through your foul schemes
Controlling the universe is way beyond your means
This is His creation, mess with it never
Repercussions you wouldn't be able to bear.

This world has had enough of your stupid ways
Meaningless War, terrorism and pollution
Now it's time to face the aftermath
Soon you are gonna be wiped out...

— Raj

98. You lost me the moment

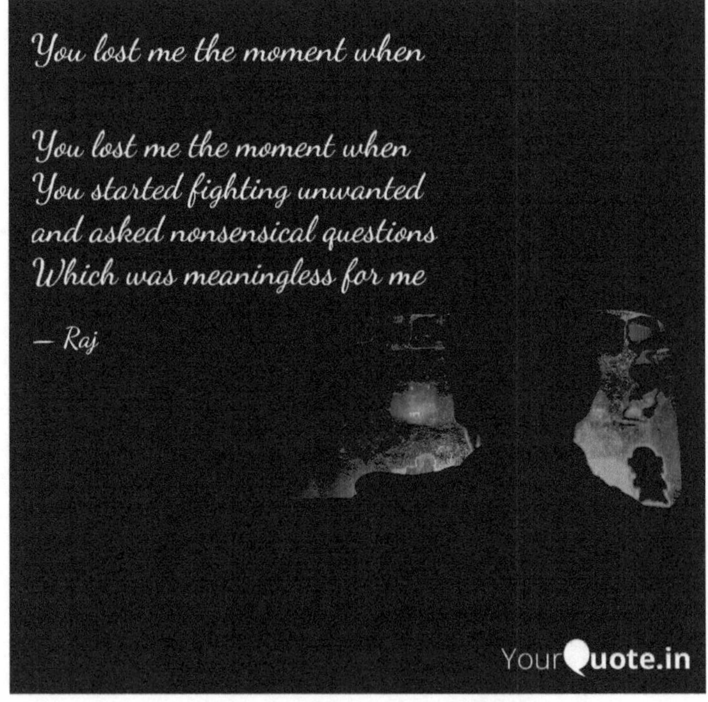

You lost me the moment when

You lost me the moment when
You started fighting unwanted
and asked nonsensical questions
Which was meaningless for me

— Raj

99. You're that art

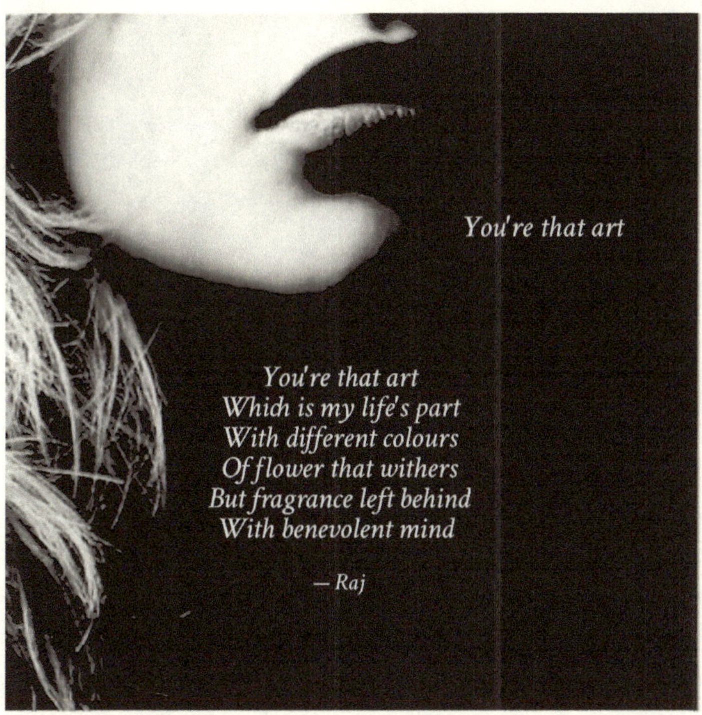

You're that art

You're that art
Which is my life's part
With different colours
Of flower that withers
But fragrance left behind
With benevolent mind

— Raj

100. You can't control life

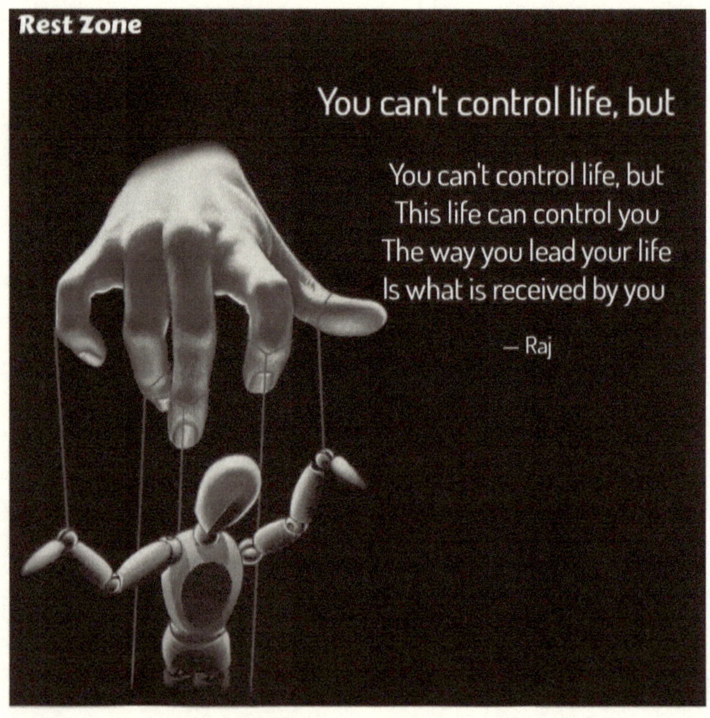

Rest Zone
You can't control life, but

You can't control life, but
This life can control you
The way you lead your life
Is what is received by you

— Raj

Disclaimer

All creations are my own creations and based on fiction. It has nothing to do with the life of the author or anyone in the universe. All articles are fictitious and bear no resemblance to any person living or dead. If there is any similarity, it is just coincidence.

Authors Bio

Mr. K. C. Shreeraj Menon born to an affluent family in Kerala on 09th September 1973 to Mr. Kozhipurath Sankunni Menon and Mrs. Kizhara Chalapurath Sethulakshmi Menon and Domiciled in Maharashtra. From childhood, he used to make quick poetry, say and forget it. A close friend of his once noticed this and forced him to write whatever Poems or Quotes he used to say and since then he started writing. He kept his poetry and Quotes to himself and his close friends until he found a platform to write his works online. He is an active writer on Your Quote site and has received numerous testimonials and certifications for the contest. He is a multilingual writer and his writing is awe-inspiring. Be it English, Hindi, Urdu, Malayalam and Marathi, he excels in all languages. He is also a great inspiration to many intriguing writers. He is a graduate from Mumbai University. He is an accountant and also a self-educated computer engineer. His skills are top notch and he holds several certifications. His passions are acting, writing, painting and dance and listening to music etc… etc….

Mail Id:- shreeraj_m@yahoo.co.uk